Step Two

Classical Guitar Playing

Compiled and edited by
Tony Skinner and Raymond Burley

Printed and bound in Great Britain

Published by Registry Publications

Registry House, Churchill Mews, Dennett Rd, Croydon, CR0 3JH

Cover guitars: Rohan Lowe, John Price, Martin Fleeson

A CIP record for this publication is available from the British Library
ISBN: 1-898466-60-2

Compiled for **LCM Exams** by

INTRODUCTION

This publication is part of a progressive series of ten handbooks, primarily intended for candidates considering taking the London College Of Music examinations in classical guitar playing. However, given each handbook's wide content of musical repertoire, and associated educational material, the series provides a solid foundation of musical education for any classical guitar student – whether intending to take an examination or not. Whilst the handbooks can be used for independent study, they are ideally intended as a supplement to individual or group tuition.

Examination entry

An examination entry form is provided at the rear of each handbook. This is the only valid entry form for the London College Of Music classical guitar examinations.

Please note that *if the entry form is detached and lost, it will not be replaced under any circumstances* and the candidate will be required to obtain a replacement handbook to obtain another entry form.

Editorial information

All performance pieces should be played in full, including all repeats shown. The pieces have been edited specifically for examination use, with all non-required repeat markings omitted. Examination performances must be from this handbook edition. Tempos, fingering, and dynamic markings are for general guidance only and need not be rigidly adhered to.

Right-hand fingering is normally shown on the stem side of the notes:
p = thumb; *i* = index; *m* = middle; *a* = third.

Left-hand fingering is shown with the numbers **1 2 3 4**, normally to the left side of the note head.
0 indicates an open string.

String numbers are shown in a circle, normally below the note. For example, ⑥ = 6th string.

Arpeggiated chords (i.e. broken or spread chords) that are strummed, normally with the thumb, are indicated by a vertical wavy line to the left of the chord – with an arrowhead showing the direction of the strum.

Acknowledgements

The editors acknowledge the help of the many libraries and copyright owners that facilitated access to original manuscripts, source materials and facsimiles during the compilation of this series of books. The editors are grateful for the advice and support of all the members of the Registry Of Guitar Tutors 'Classical Guitar Advisory Panel', and are particularly indebted for the expertise and contributions of:

Carlos Bonell Hon.RCM, Chris Ackland GRSM LRAM LTCL,
Chaz Hart LRAM, Frank Bliven BM MA, Alan J. Brown LTCL.

SECTION ONE – FINGERBOARD KNOWLEDGE

The examiner may ask you to play *from memory* any of the scales or chords shown below. Scales should be played ascending and descending, i.e. from the lowest note to the highest and back again, without a pause and without repeating the top note. Chords should be played ascending only, and sounded string by string, starting with the lowest (root) note. To achieve a legato (i.e. smooth and over-ringing) sound, the whole chord shape should be placed on the fingerboard before, and kept on during, playing. Chords should be played tirando, i.e. using free strokes.

To allow for flexibility in teaching approaches, the right and left hand recommended fingering suggestions given below are *not* compulsory and alternative systematic fingerings, that are musically effective, will be accepted. Suggested tempos are for general guidance only. Slightly slower or faster performances will be acceptable, providing that the tempo is maintained evenly throughout.

Overall, the examiner will be listening for accurate, even and clear playing. Pressing with the tips of the left-hand fingers, as close to the fretwire as possible, will aid clarity.

A maximum of 25 marks may be awarded in this section of the examination.

Recommended right hand fingering and tempo

Scales: alternating *i m*;   tirando (free stroke) or apoyando (rest stroke) tempo ♩ = 112
Chords: *p* - on all bass strings,   tirando   tempo ♩ = 152
   i m a - on the treble strings;

C Major scale - 1 octave   G Major scale - 1 octave

A Harmonic Minor scale - 1 octave   E Harmonic Minor scale - 1 octave

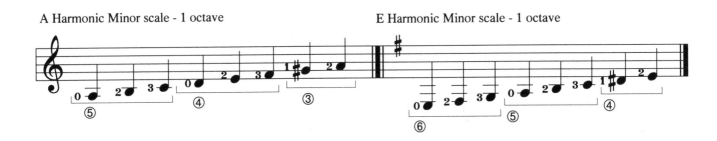

G Major chord   E Minor chord

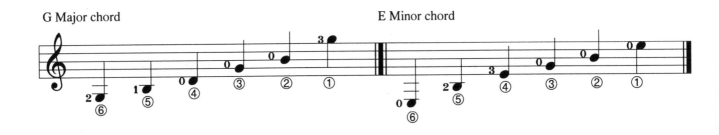

SECTION TWO – PERFORMANCE

Candidates should play any *two* melodies from group A, plus any *one* piece from group B.

A maximum of 60 marks may be awarded in this section of the examination – i.e. up to 20 marks for each performance.

Tempo markings are for general guidance only and do not need to be adhered to strictly. All repeat markings should be followed.

Performance Tips

Melodies:

- The melodies are all in the key of G major. This means that the notes contained in the melodies will all be taken from the G major scale, shown in Section One of this handbook; the only exceptions being some notes that, whilst still within the key, are just beyond the range of the one octave scale. It would be helpful preparation to thoroughly study the G major scale before starting to play any of these melodies.

- Suggestions for right-hand fingering are given in the first few bars of each melody.

- The first three melodies all include *first and second time endings*: the bars bracketed as ⌐1. should be omitted on the repeat playing and replaced with those bracketed as ⌐2.

- The *William Tell* theme should be played at a brisk tempo to capture the lively spirit of the piece.

Malagueña:

- Don't be put of by the difficult looking chords in the first two bars: both chords require only two fretted notes. Once you have learnt the chord shapes, they'll prove very useful – particularly as the first chord shape (E major) occurs many times throughout the piece as a 'spread chord', such as in bars 5 and 15.

- Be careful not to rush the first few bars, or you'll find it very difficult to maintain the tempo once the quaver section begins from bar 15.

- In bars 15 to 22, the melody lies in the bass and should be played throughout with the thumb. The repeated open high E string is there just to give a sense of movement and contrast; it should not be played too loudly.

- The key signature is A minor, although in this typical Spanish style the harmonic emphasis is on the dominant chord (E major).

Double O Waltz:

- The key signature is E minor.

- Start quite softly in order to create the mood of mystery that the beginning of this piece requires.

- From bar 13 onwards the tone should be quite strong, with a steady tempo to capture the rhythmical waltz feel of this section.

- The arpeggiated chord in the final bar should be strummed strongly with the thumb in order to create a dramatic ending. The fermata (pause sign) above the chord indicates that the chord should be left to ring-on for longer than its normal duration.

Autumn Sunshine:

- This piece uses a repeated *p i m a* right-hand finger pattern.

- The melody lies in the bass and should be brought out clearly.

- The treble strings should not be played too loudly, except in bars 5 and 6 where the higher notes at the end of each set of four quavers should be held and emphasised slightly (as indicated by the *tenuto* lines).

- The marking '*rall.*' under the final bar is an abbreviation for *rallentando,* which means 'gradually play slower'.

- The key signature is E minor.

Lenimento:

- The key signature is C major.

- The piece begins with a C major chord and the first two bars use a *p i m a m* right-hand finger pattern, which re-occurs in bars 5 and 6.

- The title suggests the style of a slow lament. In order to achieve the smooth legato sound that suits this style, all the notes within each bar, particularly the bass notes, should be held on throughout the bar whenever possible. A warm gentle tone should be used.

- At the end of bar 9, the piece should be started again from the beginning – omitting bar 9 on the second playing and proceeding straight to the second-time ending.

Spring

[Group A]

Antonio Vivaldi
(1678 – 1741)

Minuet

[Group A]

Johann Sebastian Bach
(1685 – 1750)

Là Ci Darem La Mano

Wolfgang Amadeus Mozart
(1756 - 1791)

[Group A]

William Tell Overture

Gioacchino Rossini
(1792 - 1868)

[Group A]

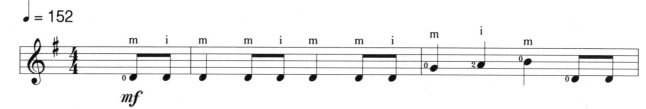

Malagueña

[Group B]

Traditional Spanish

Double O Waltz

Lawrence Sabor
(1950 - 2001)

[Group B]

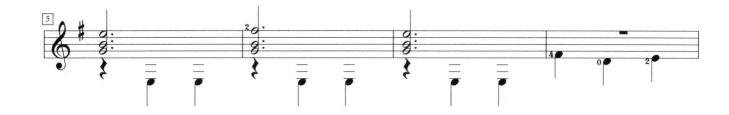

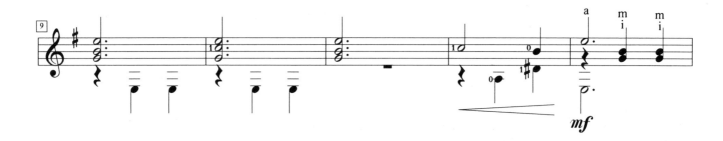

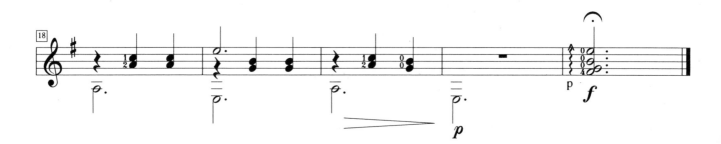

Autumn Sunshine

[Group B]

Tony Skinner
(1960 -)

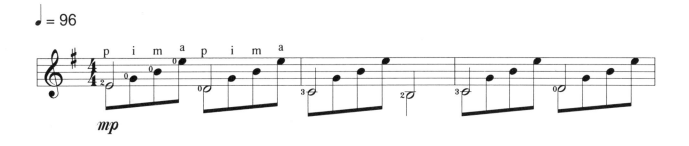

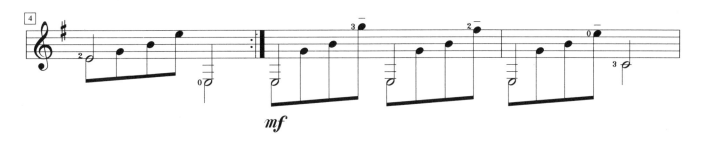

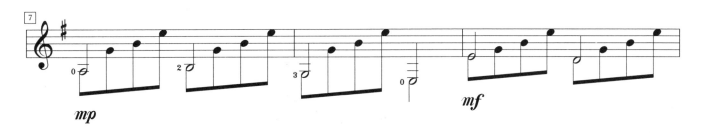

Lenimento

[Group B]

Gerard Ward
(1963 -)

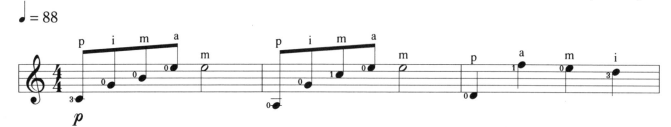

© Copyright 2001 by Registry Publications

SECTION 3 – MUSICAL KNOWLEDGE

A maximum of 15 marks may be awarded in this section of the examination.

The examiner will ask questions, based on the music performed, to test the candidate's knowledge of the stave, bar lines, notes and rests, key and time signatures, accidentals and dynamics. The information below provides a summary of the information that is required.

The stave

The notes on the lines (E G B D F) can be remembered by making up an unusual phrase such as: <u>E</u>normous <u>G</u>uitarists <u>B</u>reak <u>D</u>ainty <u>F</u>ootstools. The notes in the spaces between the lines form the word FACE.

Bar lines

A bar is a way of dividing music into manageable portions. The end of each bar is indicated by a vertical line called a *bar line*. The space between each pair of bar lines, where the notes are written, is called a *bar* (also known as a *measure*). At the end of a piece, or section, of music there are two vertical lines. These are called a *double bar line*.

Notes and rests

The table below shows the names of the notes and rests, and their values.

Traditional name	Modern name	Note	Rest	Value in crotchet beats
semibreve	whole note	𝅝	▬	4
dotted minim	dotted half note	𝅗𝅥.	▬.	3
minim	half note	𝅗𝅥	▬	2
crotchet	quarter note	♩	𝄽	1
quaver	eighth note	♪	𝄾	½

Time signatures

The numbers that appear at the beginning of a piece of music are called the time signature. The top number shows the number of beats per bar, whilst the bottom number indicates the value of each beat. For example, $^4_4$ means four crotchet beats (i.e. four quarter notes) per bar, whilst $^3_4$ means three crotchet beats per bar.

2 crotchet beats per bar.   3 crotchet beats per bar.   4 crotchet beats per bar.

Key signatures

Where there is one sharp at the beginning of each stave of a piece of music, this indicates that the key is either G major or E minor. You can often establish whether the key is major or minor by looking at the first and final notes of the piece. For example, in a piece with a key signature of one sharp, if the first and last note is E (as in *Autumn Sunshine*) then it is likely that the piece is in the key of E minor, rather than G major.

- When one sharp occurs in a key signature it will always be on the top F line, and indicates that all F notes throughout the piece should be played as F#.

- Where there is no visible key signature the key will be C major or A minor.

A sharp or flat that occurs during a piece of music, rather than as part of the key signature, is called an **accidental**. It has the effect of sharpening or flattening just that one note, and any others at the same pitch within the same bar. It does not affect notes in the following bars.

The appearance of an accidental can often indicate a minor key. For example, the occurrence of a D# note in bar 12 of *Double O Waltz* confirms the key signature as E minor. (Whilst the G major scale contains the note D, the E harmonic minor scale contains D#).

C Major or A Minor

G Major or E Minor

Dynamic markings

Dynamic markings indicate how softly or strongly to play:

p is short for *piano* – meaning 'soft' (quiet).

f is short for *forte* – meaning 'strong' (loud).

m is short for 'mezzo' (i.e. half) – meaning 'moderately'. *m* does not occur on its own, but can be combined with *f* or *p*: *mf* means 'moderately strong', *mp* means 'moderately soft'.

This sign ⟨ means *crescendo* (get louder).

This sign ⟩ means *diminuendo* (get quieter).

London College of **Music** & **Media**
THAMES VALLEY UNIVERSITY

Examination Entry Form
for
Classical Guitar

STEP TWO

PLEASE COMPLETE CLEARLY IN INK AND IN BLOCK CAPITAL LETTERS

SESSION (Spring/Summer/Winter): _____ YEAR: _____

Preferred Examination Centre (if known): _____
If left blank you will examined at the nearest venue to your home address.

Candidate Details:

Candidate Name (as to appear on certificate):

_____

Address: _____

_____ Postcode: _____

Tel. No. (day): _____ (evening): _____

Tick this box if you are also entering for LCM Theory of Music ☐
If so, which Grade? _____

Teacher Details:

Teacher Name (as to appear on certificate): _____

LCM Teacher Code (if entered previously): _____

RGT Tutor Code (if applicable): _____

Address: _____

_____ Postcode: _____

Tel. No. (day): _____ (evening): _____

Tick this box if any details above have changed since your last LCM entry ☐

Tick this box if the teacher has also entered pupils for ☐
RGT Electric or Bass Guitar examinations for the same session.

IMPORTANT NOTES

- It is the candidate's responsibility to have knowledge of, and comply with, the current syllabus requirements. Where candidates are entered for examinations by a teacher, the teacher must take responsibility that candidates are entered in accordance with the current syllabus requirements. Failure to carry out any of the examination requirements may lead to disqualification.
- For candidates with special needs, a letter giving details, and medical certificate as appropriate, should be attached.
- Any practical appointment requests (e.g. 'prefer morning,' or 'prefer weekdays') must be made at the time of entry. **LCM and its Representatives will take note of the information given, however, no guarantees can be made that all wishes will be met.**
- Submission of this entry is an undertaking to abide by the current regulations as listed in the current syllabus and any subsequent regulations updates published in the LCM Examinations Newsletter issued each term.
- Entries for public centres should be sent **to the LCM local representative**. Contact the LCM office for details of your nearest centre or to enquire about setting up your own centre.

Examination Fee   £ _____

Late Entry Fee (if necessary)   £ _____

Total amount submitted   £ _____
Cheques or postal orders should be made payable to **'Thames Valley University'**.

A current list of fees and entry deadlines is available from LCM Exams.

LCM Exams
Thames Valley University
St Mary's Road
London
W5 5RF

Tel: 020 8231 2364
Fax: 020 8231 2433

e-mail: lcm.exams@tvu.ac.uk

The standard LCM music entry form is NOT valid for Classical Guitar entries. **Entry to the examination is only possible via this original form. Photocopies of this form will not be accepted under any circumstances.**

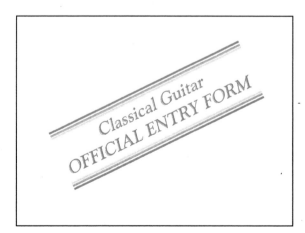